ANIMAL IDIOMS

Sly as a Fox: Are Foxes Clever?

BY MARIE-THERESE MILLER

CONTENT CONSULTANT
DAVID DRAKE, PhD
PROFESSOR AND EXTENSION WILDLIFE SPECIALIST
UNIVERSITY OF WISCONSIN, MADISON

Kids Core
An Imprint of Abdo Publishing
abdobooks.com

abdobooks.com

Printed in the United States of America, North Mankato, Minnesota.
102021
012022

THIS BOOK CONTAINS RECYCLED MATERIALS

Cover Photo: Kostya Zatulin/Shutterstock Images
Interior Photos: Roshizawati Hamza/Shutterstock Images, 4–5; Eric Isselee/Shutterstock Images, 7 (top left), 7 (top center); Shutterstock Images, 7 (top right), 8, 12, 24; Jay Pierstorff/Shutterstock Images, 7 (bottom left); Rafael Martos Martins/Shutterstock Images, 7 (bottom right); Andrew Molinaro/Shutterstock Images, 7 (bottom center); Rejean Bedard/Shutterstock Images, 10–11; Bardzo Photo/Shutterstock Images, 14; Michelle Holihan/Shutterstock Images, 16–17; Zdenek Machacek/Shutterstock Images, 18; Jakub Rutkiewicz/Shutterstock Images, 19; Holly S. Cannon/Shutterstock Images, 20; Stanislav Duben/Shutterstock Images, 22–23; Holly Kuchera/Shutterstock Images, 25; Lukas Zeman Photos/Shutterstock Images, 26; Andrew Balcombe/Shutterstock Images, 28 (bottom); Sam Chad/iStockphoto, 28 (top); Evelyn D. Harrison/Shutterstock Images, 29 (top); Rejean Bedard/iStockphoto, 29 (bottom)

Editor: Christine Ha
Series Designer: Katharine Hale

Library of Congress Control Number: 2021941210

Publisher's Cataloging-in-Publication Data

Names: Miller, Marie-Therese, author.
Title: Sly as a fox: are foxes clever? / by Marie-Therese Miller
Other title: are foxes clever?
Description: Minneapolis, Minnesota : Abdo Publishing, 2022 | Series: Animal idioms | Includes online resources and index.
Identifiers: ISBN 9781532196706 (lib. bdg.) | ISBN 9781644946497 (pbk.) | ISBN 9781098218515 (ebook)
Subjects: LCSH: Foxes--Juvenile literature. | Foxes--Behavior--Juvenile literature. | Animal intelligence--Juvenile literature. | Animal instinct--Juvenile literature. | Idiomatic expressions--Juvenile literature.
Classification: DDC 599.775--dc23

CONTENTS

Greyson found a very clever hiding spot for his stuffed fox.

CHAPTER 1

Sly Foxes

Lily and Greyson decide to play hide-and-seek. Greyson will hide his stuffed fox Ferne for Lily to find.

Lily closes her eyes and counts to 50. Greyson finds a great hiding spot for Ferne. Then, Lily searches for the small stuffed fox.

She looks behind chairs and under tables. She even peeks in the bathtub. But she can't find Ferne!

"I give up," Lily says. "I can't find her anywhere!" Greyson grins. He leads Lily to a pile of stuffed toys. Ferne is sitting right on top.

"You hid Ferne in an obvious spot, but I still didn't see her! You are sly as a fox, Greyson!" Lily says.

Fox Communication

Foxes use a variety of sounds to communicate. This includes yips, growls, barks, and howls. Foxes can also recognize and tell each other's voices apart.

Types of Foxes

Examples of True Foxes

Red fox

Arctic fox

Fennec fox

Examples of Other Foxes

Gray fox

Bat-eared fox

Crab-eating fox

The term *fox* describes small- to medium-sized doglike animals with bushy tails, pointed ears, and narrow snouts. While there are about 37 animals called foxes, there are only 12 true foxes. These foxes belong to the genus *Vulpes*. A genus is a grouping of animals that share common characteristics.

Foxes come in many colors and sizes.

What Are Idioms?

Sly as a fox is an idiom. An idiom is an expression that is often used in a specific language. It usually means something other than the words that make up the idiom. *Sly as a fox* describes someone who is clever.

But are foxes clever? The answer is yes! Foxes find places to live and food to eat in **resourceful** ways. Foxes also outsmart animals that are hunting them.

Primary Source

Aesop's Fables were written to teach lessons. In one story, a fox tricks a crow out of its breakfast:

> "What a charming creature she is!" said the Fox [about the crow]. "Such a wonderful bird should have a very lovely voice. . . ."
>
> Listening to these flattering words, the Crow [cawed], and down fell the cheese straight into the Fox's open mouth.

Source: "The Fox & the Crow." *Library of Congress Aesop Fables*, n.d., read.gov. Accessed 29 June 2021.

What's the Big Idea?

Read the fable carefully. What is its main idea? Explain how the main idea is supported by details, naming two or three of those supporting details.

Red foxes are the largest of the true foxes. They can reach a length of about 4 feet (1.2 m) from head to tail.

CHAPTER 2

Resourceful Foxes

Red foxes are the most widespread type of fox. They are found in North America, Europe, Asia, North Africa, and Australia. They live in many different types of habitats, such as grasslands, forests, mountains, and deserts.

Although foxes can be social and live in family groups, they will hunt and forage for food alone.

Red foxes are **adaptable** in many ways. For example, some red foxes have adjusted to living near people. Some live near farms and in suburbs. These foxes sometimes make their dens under barns, below outdoor sheds, or on golf courses. Red foxes even live in cities with lots of humans around them. Some live in New York City's Central Park!

Foxes and Food

Red foxes are omnivores. This means they eat both animals and plants. They hunt small animals, such as rabbits, voles, and mice.

Saving for Later

Many foxes bury extra food to dig up later in the winter or when food is harder to find. They take great care in hiding their food. They cover the food up with soil, grass, or snow. This behavior is called caching.

Foxes can be found in many big cities. For example, in 2020, the nature conservation charity London Wildlife Trust estimated that approximately 10,000 foxes lived in London.

They eat birds and their eggs, as well as insects. Foxes also eat berries and nuts.

Red foxes that live near humans get food from people. They dig through garbage to find things to eat. They also eat pet food left outside. Foxes may even eat fruit planted in people's gardens and orchards.

Further Evidence

Visit the website below. Does it give further evidence to support Chapter Two?

Red Fox

abdocorelibrary.com/sly-as-a-fox

The way a fox hunts depends on the environment it's in and the type of prey it hunts.

CHAPTER 3

How Foxes Hunt

Red foxes spend much of their time hunting. They often hunt at twilight or dawn, but they hunt at night too. These are the times that their **prey** animals are most active. Red foxes usually hunt alone. This way they can quietly sneak up on their prey.

Red foxes usually claim an area as their hunting territory. This area is usually 5 square miles (13 sq km) or smaller.

They creep up on small animals and **pounce** on them.

Red foxes use their excellent senses of sight, hearing, and smell to locate prey. They can

Locations with humans usually have many sources of food for foxes to find.

hear prey from far away. They have slit-shaped pupils to help them hunt in dim light. Foxes also have a good sense of smell that helps them know when prey is near.

Ears for Hunting

Red foxes have large ears and excellent hearing. This lets the foxes hear small prey under leaves, snow, or underground. Red foxes can hear up to 150 feet (45.7 m) away! Their hearing also helps them avoid **predators**.

In the winter, arctic foxes' white fur helps them blend into the snow. This makes them hard to spot for both prey and predators.

When red foxes hunt, they sometimes use human-made paths. This makes traveling easier. They might follow hiking trails, roads, or **irrigation** ditches.

Arctic Foxes and Hunting

Arctic foxes live in areas of the Northern Hemisphere, such as Alaska and Greenland. During the winter months, food is hard to find. The foxes may follow polar bears to steal some of their kills. An arctic fox will wait until the polar bear has left its kill to take any remaining meat. This is risky because polar bears can eat arctic foxes!

Explore Online

Visit the website below. Does it give any new information about arctic foxes that wasn't in Chapter Three?

Arctic Fox

abdocorelibrary.com/sly-as-a-fox

While a coyote is a fox's predator, coyotes rarely hunt adult foxes for food. Instead, they often target foxes to eliminate hunting competition.

CHAPTER 4

Escape Artists

Wolves, golden eagles, owls, and coyotes are predators of red foxes. But red foxes are great at escaping them. Red foxes can run up to 30 miles per hour (48 km/h)! They may run through water so predators cannot follow their smell.

They sometimes run back the same way they came to confuse the predator.

Crafty Dens

Red foxes, like many other types of foxes, give birth to their kits in dens. Sometimes they dig their own dens in the ground. But many times, they save themselves the work. They take over unused dens of other animals. They often dig

Foxes use dens as places to raise their kits and store food.

The gray fox is also known as the tree fox.

more than one entrance. This lets them escape if a predator finds them.

Tree Climbers

Though gray foxes are not true foxes, they are also clever. Gray foxes are found in North America and northern South America. They have long, hooked claws on their back feet and flexible front legs. These features help them climb trees easily. They can even climb down trees backward.

In legends around the world, foxes are often clever and powerful tricksters.

Gray foxes forage for small animals and fruit in trees. When they are in danger, they climb trees to escape predators. Sometimes, gray foxes even make their homes in trees. They can live up to 30 feet (9.1 m) off the ground.

So, is *sly as a fox* an accurate expression? Are foxes clever? Yes, they are! Foxes are resourceful creatures. They live all over the world in all types of habitats. Different types of foxes have clever ways to hunt and escape predators.

Primary Source

In an interview, Richard Gray learned from ecologist Max Allen how clever foxes can be:

> Gray foxes . . . have been filmed . . . rubbing themselves in the scent marks left by mountain lions. They may be using the scent . . . as a sort of odor camouflage against other large predators such as coyotes.

Source: Richard Gray. "Foxes May Confuse Predators." *NewScientist*, 19 Jan. 2017, newscientist.com. Accessed 30 June 2021.

Comparing Texts

Does the quote support the information in this chapter? Or does it give a different perspective? Explain how in a few sentences.

Fox Facts

Arctic foxes sometimes follow polar bears and steal a bit of their kills to eat.

Red foxes take advantage of living near humans to find food in garbage cans and gardens.

Gray foxes climb trees to find prey and to escape predators.

Foxes often use dens abandoned by other animals instead of making their own.

Glossary

adaptable
able to change behavior in different situations

irrigation
the process of watering crops through human-made means, such as pipes

pounce
to jump forward and grab something suddenly

predators
animals that hunt other animals for food

prey
animals that are hunted by other animals for food

resourceful
able to find clever ways to solve problems

Online Resources

To learn more about foxes, visit our free resource websites below.

Core Library CONNECTION
FREE! COMMON CORE MULTIMEDIA RESOURCES

Visit **abdocorelibrary.com** or scan this QR code for free Common Core resources for teachers and students, including vetted activities, multimedia, and booklinks, for deeper subject comprehension.

Booklinks NONFICTION NETWORK
FREE! ONLINE NONFICTION RESOURCES

Visit **abdobooklinks.com** or scan this QR code for free additional online weblinks for further learning. These links are routinely monitored and updated to provide the most current information available.

Learn More

Alkire, Jessie. *Arctic Foxes.* Abdo, 2019.

Grady, Tyler. *Red Fox.* Dylanna Publishing, 2021.

Ventura, Marne. *Lazy as a Dog: Are Dogs Sluggish?* Abdo, 2022.

Index

About the Author

Marie-Therese Miller is the author of nonfiction books for children and teens. She has written the Dog Tales series, *Rachel Carson*, *Rock Climbing*, the Many Ways series, and three books in the Sesame Street Character Guides series. Miller earned her PhD in English from St. John's University. She teaches Children's and YA Literature at Marist College, the home of the Red Foxes. Miller and her husband, John, have five children and a grandson.